DESERTS

Hundreds of years ago, camels went across the Sahara Desert with salt on their backs, and travellers told stories about the city of Timbuktu. People rode horses across the cold Gobi Desert, and the big saguaro cactus plants of the Sonoran Desert slowly grew bigger and bigger.

These things happen today – but the desert is changing. There are camels, but there are also 4x4s in the desert. There are travellers to Timbuktu, but now they come to take photographs and listen to music.

And there are new treasures out there in the desert – energy from the hot sun, and food plants that can grow in hot dry places. Perhaps we need to look at the desert with new eyes . . .

OXFORD BOOKWORMS LIBRARY
Factfiles

Deserts

Stage 1 (400 headwords)

Factfiles Series Editor: Christine Lindop

JANET HARDY-GOULD

Deserts

OXFORD UNIVERSITY PRESS

1

and education by publishing worldwide in

Oxford New York

Auckland Cape Town Dar es Salaam Hong Kong Karachi
Kuala Lumpur Madrid Melbourne Mexico City Nairobi
New Delhi Shanghai Taipei Toronto

With offices in

Argentina Austria Brazil Chile Czech Republic France Greece
Guatemala Hungary Italy Japan Poland Portugal Singapore
South Korea Switzerland Thailand Turkey Ukraine Vietnam

OXFORD and OXFORD ENGLISH are registered trade marks of
Oxford University Press in the UK and in certain other countries

ISBN: 978 0 19 423627 0

A complete recording of this Bookworms edition of *Deserts*
is available on audio CD ISBN 978 0 19 423628 7

Printed in China

Word count (main text): 5,519

For more information on the Oxford Bookworms Library,
visit www.oup.com/bookworms

ACKNOWLEDGEMENTS

Cover image by: Getty Images (Namib desert/Franck Guiziou/hemis.fr)

Illustration pp2–3 by: Gareth Riddiford

The publishers would like to thank the following for their kind permission to reproduce photographs:
africanpictures.net pp9 (Bushmen grass homestead, Kalahari/Ariadne Van Zandbergen), 24 (Afar mine
salt for the 'salt caravan'/Ariadne Van Zandbergen); Ardea p17 (Scorpion/Karl Terblanche); Axiom
Photographic Agency p10 (Tuareg nomad/Alberto Arzoz); FLPA pp14 (Paper daisies/Krystyna Szulecka),
15 (Jerboa/Arthur Christiansen), 16 (Fennec fox/Michael Mährlein), 17 (Black Vulture/William S. Clark);
fotolibra.com p30 (Tinariwen, festival in the desert/Edwina Sassoon); Getty Images pp12 (Saguaro cactus/
Carr Clifton); 12 (Giant Saguaro cactus/Yva Momatiuk/John Eastcott); 17 (Shovel-snouted Lizard/Michael
& Patricia Fogden), 20 (Bedouin goatherd/National Geographic); 23 (Bedouin man pours coffee/National
Geographic); ImageState pp19 (Bedouin sheikh in his tent/Piers Cavendish / Impact Photos), 29 (16th
century Koran manuscripts/Robert Berger); National Geographic Image Collection p34 (Joshua tree in
bloom/Tim Laman); Newspix p39 (Panasonic World Solar Challenge/News Ltd/3rd Party Managed
Reproduction & Supply Rights); OUP pp44 (oil), 44 (cactus/Photodisc), 44 (Date palm/Photodisc),
44 (sand dune/Corbis/Digital Stock), 44 (lizard/Corbis/Digital Stock), 44 (Camel and rider/Corbis/Digital
Stock); Oz Images pviii (Desert sunset/S. Cyd Read of Natural Born Hikers); Panos Pictures pp25 (Workers
at an oil field in Southern Algeria/Sven Torfinn), 27 (Government buildings Saudi Arabia/Jeremy Horner);
Photolibrary p5 (sand dunes Namib Desert/moodboard); Robert Harding Picture Library pp4 (The Siq,
Petra/Neale Clark), 6 (Umm El Ma lake/Sergio Pitamitz), 13 (Date palm/Sylvain Grandadam), 18 (Camel
at the Khongryn dunes/Bruno Morandi), 31 (Sahara landscape/Sylvain Grandadam); Still Pictures
pp8 (Tuareg at homestead/McPhoto), 11 (Indian woman with clay pot/J.Royan), 26 (copper mine/
(Freelans Pool) Tack), 28 (Sankore mosque/McPhoto), 33 (traditional yurts/Hartmut Schwarzbach/argus),
35 (Mummy archaeological museum/Biosphoto/Dani Carlo & Jeske Ingrid), 37 (Erosion/Mark Edwards),
38 (Sand boarder/Paul Springett), 40 (Solar energy plant/Wildlife/T.Dressler).*

CONTENTS

1   What is a desert?

When you find a photo of a desert in a book, it is usually a very hot, dry place with a lot of yellow sand and no animals or people. Is this a true picture of deserts across the world? The answer is yes – and no.

Deserts are, of course, very dry – a desert has under 25 centimetres of rain every year. In some deserts there is no rain for a very long time. In the Atacama Desert in South America, for example, there was rain in 1971 – but before that there was no rain for 400 years.

Deserts are dry – but are they always hot? Think of the Arabian Desert with its temperatures of up to 50 °C, and you want to say yes. But some deserts are hot for only part of the year, with very cold winters. For example, temperatures in the cold Gobi Desert in China and Mongolia can go down to -30 °C in January and you can sometimes find snow there.

And hot deserts can be very cold at night too. In the Sahara, there are often temperatures of more than 38 °C in the day, but at night they can suddenly go down. In winter, some places in the Sahara are 0 °C at night.

Some people also call Antarctica a big desert, because it is dry with not much rain or snow every year. But it is very different from other deserts because it never gets hot.

Most deserts are far from the sea. The hot, dry Simpson

Desert in Australia is thousands of kilometres from the sea. But the cool Namib Desert in Africa is next to the Atlantic Ocean. There, winds come in from across the sea and change the climate.

And what about sand? Are the world's deserts all sand? Interestingly, the answer is no. About three-quarters of the desert in the world is without any sand. Much of it only has small rocks.

There are lots of people in the desert too. Millions of

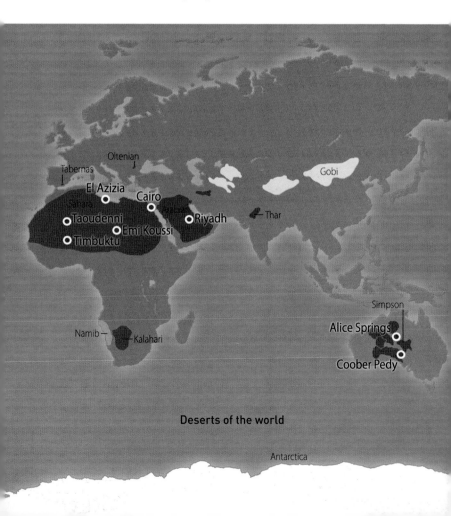

Deserts of the world

people across the world live in deserts. Many of them live in cities in very dry places – think of Las Vegas in the USA or Cairo in Egypt. Others, like the Bedouin people of the Arabian Desert and the Tuareg of the Sahara, live in and move across the world's deserts.

So perhaps deserts are different sometimes from the photos in books. Hot, cold, or cool, deserts are very important to the world. Over one quarter of the world is desert. That's a lot!

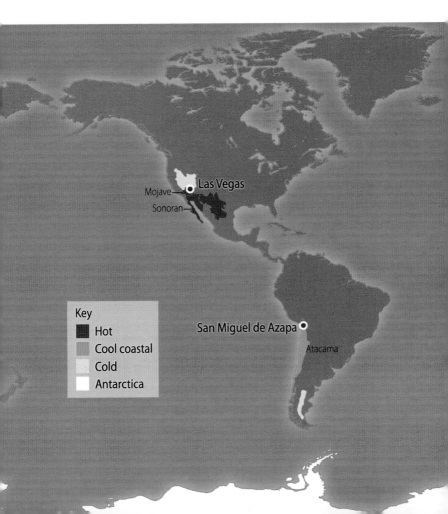

Key
■ Hot
■ Cool coastal
□ Cold
□ Antarctica

Mojave
Las Vegas
Sonoran

San Miguel de Azapa
Atacama

2 Rocks, wind, water

When people think of a desert, they often think of a place with no hills or mountains. But across many of the world's deserts you can find tall mountains and open ravines. About a quarter of the Sahara Desert has mountains. The biggest of these is Emi Koussi in Chad at 3,445 metres. For part of the year you can see snow on it.

Visitors to the Mojave Desert in California can find beautiful yellow and orange ravines. When there is a lot of rain there, the water goes into small fast rivers. Over many years, these rivers make deep ravines in the rocks.

A deep ravine

Tall sand dunes

Rocks are a very important part of many deserts. For example, much of the Gobi, the world's third biggest desert, is just rocks, with not many plants or trees.

And of course, we cannot forget sand. You can find it in deserts all over the world. But what is sand and where does it come from? Over thousands of years the weather in the desert slowly breaks huge rocks into smaller and smaller rocks. In the end, there is nothing but very, very small rocks – and this is sand.

The desert wind often moves the sand into hills, called dunes. These dunes can sometimes be very big. The Namib Desert in Africa has some of the tallest dunes in the world, at 380 metres or more.

Wind not only makes sand dunes but it can also move them across the desert. Over time, the wind blows sand from the front part of the dune to the back. Because of this a dune can move between 20 and 30 metres every year. When the sand moves it sometimes makes a singing noise! The people of the Sahara tell old stories about *djenouns*. Djenouns are small 'people' and they sometimes sing from under the big dunes.

In some deserts there are places with a lot of salt. When it rains, the salt comes out of the rocks and goes into the water. The water then quickly evaporates in the hot temperatures, but leaves the salt on the desert.

But not all water in the desert evaporates quickly. You can find water in an oasis. The water there often comes

An oasis in North Africa

up from rivers deep under the desert. The people of the desert sometimes walk or drive for a long time to find an oasis. There are many famous oases in the east of the Sahara in Egypt.

But you need to be careful when you look for an oasis. When there are very hot temperatures you can begin to see things! Hot deserts are famous for their mirages. You see a beautiful oasis with cool water – but it is a mirage. In front of you there are only kilometres of sand.

3   Desert life

Life in deserts, with their changing temperatures, warm winds and dry weather, can be very difficult. But you can find people in every hot desert across the world. For example, there are the San people of the Kalahari Desert in Africa and the Aborigines of the huge, dry deserts of Australia. These people began to live there thousands of years ago and their lives are adapted to the difficult desert climate.

Many desert people are nomads – they move from place to place and look for food and water. Some nomads have animals and they need to find food and water for them too. The Tuareg people of the Sahara, for example, move across the desert with their hungry goats and other animals.

A Tuareg tent

A grass home in the Kalahari

Nomads often take their homes with them. A traditional Tuareg home is a huge tent with a very large bed inside. Tuareg women can take down their tents and put everything away very quickly – it only takes two hours! Fifty years ago Tuaregs usually moved their tents on camels. Now they often put their homes on big cars and then drive to the next place. But like many desert people across the world, a lot of Tuaregs now live in houses next to the desert and they stay there all the time.

Not all nomads take their homes with them. In the Kalahari Desert, the San people make a home from parts of trees and plants when they stop for the night. Sometimes they move the next day to a new place, and then they make a different home that night.

And not all desert people are nomads. Some live in houses – for example in the north of India. People in the Thar Desert make their houses from sand and dry grass.

A Tuareg rider wearing
a blue scarf

These homes are nice and cool in the hot temperatures of
the day.

In Australia you can find homes *under* the desert! Many
houses in the town of Coober Pedy are built down in the
cool rock or into a hill. These homes usually have a
number of different rooms, and the temperature is always
about 24 °C.

Other things are very important too for life in the hot
desert climate. Bedouins of the Sahara wear long scarves
on their heads, so their heads stay cooler. The Tuareg
people of the Sahara are also famous for their blue
scarves. The scarves go over their heads and across their
mouths. When the wind blows sand at their faces, the
sand stays on the scarves, and they do not get sand in
their mouths.

In hot temperatures, people cannot live without water

for more than three days, so finding water is very important. Some people in the Arabian Desert walk or drive for many days when they need to find an oasis or small river. Others in the Sahara make deep holes and find water under the sand. Women in the Thar Desert sometimes walk to the nearest river and carry home water in big bottles on their heads.

Finding food can be difficult too. Some people like the Tuareg live mostly from the milk, and sometimes meat, from their animals. In Australia, traditional Aborigines eat lots of different plants and animals. They know how to find them in different places across the hot dry deserts.

**A Thar woman
carrying water**

4   Desert plants

Deserts are, of course, very dry places. But there are lots of different flowers, plants, and trees in deserts all over the world. How can they live in this difficult climate? All desert plants are adapted to the dry weather and they can live without much water. For example, plants with small leaves lose less water, and plants with very big roots can take in more water when the rain comes.

One plant with huge roots is the saguaro cactus of the Sonoran Desert in North America. The roots can sometimes grow across 13 metres of the desert but they are only 10 centimetres under the sand. When it rains, the

A saguaro cactus and its spines

Date palm

roots quickly take in the water before it evaporates. In one week the saguaro can take in 800 litres of water and the water stays inside the huge cactus for a long time. These plants can grow up to 15 metres tall!

The saguaro cactus has big spines – these are adapted leaves. Animals cannot easily eat the plant because the spines get in their mouths.

Other plants have very deep roots. These go down into the desert rocks and take in water. For example, the roots of the saxaul tree of the cold Gobi Desert can go down for 18 metres. Like many desert plants, the saxaul tree can live in places with a lot of salt.

In many places in the Gobi Desert, saxauls are the only trees. Parts of these trees have a lot of water, so they are important for the desert people. When there is no rain for a long time, the nomads can get water from these trees.

The date palm tree is also an important plant for people

Paper daisies

in hot deserts. You can often find date palms next to an oasis. One tree makes about 100 kilograms of dates every year. You can cook with them, or just eat them – they are very good! The people of the Sahara also give dates to their goats and other animals. The leaves of the date palm are good too – you can make them into things for your house.

Some desert plants live for a long time. The date palm lives up to 100 years, the saxaul tree often lives for eighty or ninety years and the saguaro cactus can live up to 200 years! But other plants live only for a very short time. One of these is the famous paper daisy flower.

The paper daisy leaves its seeds in the sand of Australian deserts. These seeds can stay there for many years and they only come to life when it rains. The plants then grow fast and make beautiful flowers. When the water evaporates from the desert, the plants begin to die and the wind blows the seeds across the sand. The paper daisy is then ready to begin its life again with the next rain.

5   Desert animals

How do animals live in the desert? They need water, of course. Some animals get it from plants. Others wait under the sand for the rains. When the land is dry again, they go back under the sand. They stay there until the next rain. And some animals, like camels, can go for a long time between one drink of water and the next one.

Then there are the changes in temperature, from very hot to very cold. In the day, many animals stay in cool places under rocks or in small holes in the sand. But at night deserts can suddenly come alive. When the sun goes down the animals put their heads above the sand and begin to look for food.

The small jerboa lives in deserts across the world.

A jerboa

Jerboas have big eyes and, like many desert animals, they can see very well at night. In the late evening, they come out of their holes and look for food – mostly seeds and plants.

Jerboas are very well adapted to life in the desert. Some jerboas do not need to drink, because they get water from their food. In the hot summer, some jerboas sleep under the sand for two or three months. Jerboas also live in cold deserts like the Gobi. Here, they sleep in their holes in the winter and stay away from the snow.

A fennec fox

Jerboas can move very fast across the sand. They have huge back legs and they can jump up to three metres in one move. They do this when they need to run away from other animals – fennec foxes, for example. At night, these foxes are also looking for food, and a jerboa is just right for a hungry fennec fox. Like jerboas, fennec foxes are well adapted to the weather in the desert. With its very big ears and white coat, the fennec fox can stay much cooler in the hot sun.

There are a lot of other living things in the desert too. Scorpions come out from under rocks at night and look for small animals. Like many desert animals, scorpions can go for months without water. They can also live for up to one year without food.

A scorpion

A lizard

A black vulture

When the sun comes up the jerboas, foxes, and scorpions go down into their cool holes and under rocks. And slowly other animals come out. In hot deserts, these animals are often adapted to the hot sand under their feet. For example, the lizards of the Kalahari can stand on only two legs at a time – when these legs get hot, they quickly jump onto the other two!

Other living things stay away from the hot sand. In the afternoon, vultures sometimes go up and up in the desert sky. The temperatures are often much cooler there and they move slowly in the wind.

In the daytime, you can also see camels in the desert. Some have one hump and are called dromedary camels. Others have two humps and are called Bactrian camels. About one in ten of the world's camels are Bactrian and a small number of them live wild in the Gobi Desert. They have very warm coats and these are important for the cold weather there.

A Bactrian camel in the Gobi

Dromedary camels do not usually live wild in deserts. Thousands of years ago, nomads began to carry things across the Arabian and Sahara Deserts on these big camels and you can see them there today.

Camels are wonderfully adapted to desert life. They can go for two or three days without water. But when they come to an oasis, they can drink 110 litres in ten minutes!

Camels have huge feet too so they do not go down in the deep desert sand. Camels also have very interesting noses! When there are sudden winds, they can close their big noses and the sand does not go in them.

6   A desert people

In the nineteenth century there were Bedouins from the Sahara to Persia. These people moved across the hot deserts with their tents and camels. But now most Bedouins live in houses in towns near the desert in countries like Syria, Egypt, and Saudi Arabia. They often live a traditional Bedouin life in their houses but they no longer move from place to place.

The Bedouins have a lot of different tribes – these are like very big families but with many more people. The most important person in the tribe is the Sheikh – he is usually the oldest man from a famous family in the tribe.

Bedouin men and women often have different lives.

A Bedouin Sheikh

The men usually go out to get money and food for the family. The women work in the house or tent – they make dinner and help with animals like camels or goats.

In earlier times, the Bedouins moved across the desert

A Bedouin woman
with her goats

in their tribes. They knew every oasis and small village for many kilometres. At night, they slept in huge black tents.

They got their food and money from life in the desert. For example, they had camels and goats and took these

from place to place. They got meat and milk from these animals, and hair from their coats too. They made the hair into tents.

Every tribe had their part of the desert. When other people wanted to go across this place, they gave money or food to the tribe. The Bedouins also helped people across the most difficult parts of the desert.

Bedouins are very famous for their food and drink. When a visitor arrives in the desert, the Bedouins always ask the person into their tent. Here, the visitor first gets some hot tea and later some traditional Bedouin food — for example, bread and meat. The Bedouins are also famous for their stories of desert life and they like to tell these to their visitors over dinner.

In the desert, traditionally Bedouins give a bed to their visitors too. When there are sudden winds, people need to stay away from the open desert for a day or two. But visitors can only stay for three nights and no more! After that they need to move to the next place.

When Bedouins are ill, they eat the leaves of desert plants or they drink camel's milk. This milk is good for many different parts of the body.

The twenty-first century is difficult for many desert people like the Bedouins. The world is changing fast and they need to change too, but they do not want to lose the traditional parts of their lives.

Tea with the Bedouin

7   Desert treasures

The desert has many different treasures. Perhaps people cannot see them at first, but when they look carefully, they can find them. Let's begin with the desert's oldest treasure – salt.

Thousands of years ago, nomads went into the Sahara and looked for salt. They often got a lot of money for it in towns and villages near the desert. Salt is also important today. In the village of Taoudenni in Mali, people take huge pieces of salt from under the desert and put them onto

Putting salt on a camel

Getting oil from the desert

their camels. Every camel can take four big pieces of the salt. They then walk hundreds of kilometres to Timbuktu or other places and get money for the white salt there.

But perhaps the most famous treasure of the desert today is black. It is oil, of course. You can find oil in different deserts of the world – the Sahara and the Arabian Desert, for example.

About a quarter of the world's oil comes from deep under the Arabian Desert. People found oil there in the 1930s. In most deserts, oil is usually deep down in the rock. People make big holes in the desert rock and take the oil out.

But oil and salt are not the only important treasures of the desert. In some deserts you can find red-brown copper. The cool Atacama Desert in Chile has got much of the world's copper. You can find the biggest and deepest open copper mine in the world here. It is a huge hole in the

The world's biggest copper mine

desert – it is 4.5 kilometres long, 3.5 kilometres wide, and 1 kilometre deep! The mine is important for the country of Chile. It brings a lot of money into the country, and a lot of people have jobs there.

One last treasure of the desert is, of course, sand. Sand is important for many different things in our lives; for example, you cannot make bottles or windows without sand. People also need it when they are making houses and other buildings.

In the Kalahari and other deserts, people make sand mines. They take the sand away and get money for it. But desert mines are not always good things. In some parts of the Kalahari near the sand mines, the huge dunes are beginning to blow away in the wind. When the sand goes, animals and plants cannot live there any more.

8   A desert city

There are many famous cities in deserts across the world. Some are very big with a lot of new buildings, like Riyadh in Saudi Arabia. Riyadh has over 4 million people, about twenty hospitals, and over sixty big shopping centres. Other towns like Alice Springs in the Australian desert are much smaller. 'Alice' has about 24,000 people, one hospital and two shopping centres.

But perhaps the most famous desert city of them all is Timbuktu. Sometimes people say: 'I went to Timbuktu and back'. They did not go to Timbuktu, of course. They want to say: 'I went to a place far away and it felt like the end of the world!'

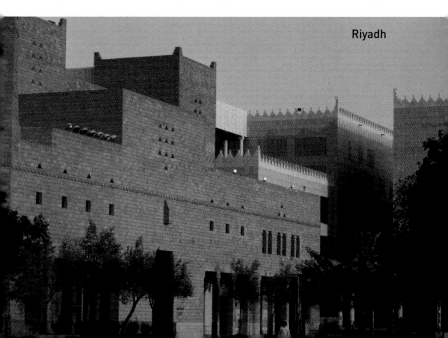

Riyadh

The University of Sankore

Timbuktu is in the south-west of the Sahara Desert in the country of Mali. Now it is a quiet city with about 20,000 people. But it also has a lot of wonderful big buildings, because long ago it was very rich and famous.

Timbuktu is nearly nine hundred years old. It began to be rich in the fourteenth century because important roads in the Sahara met there. From the north people brought salt on their camels. From the south people brought gold. And in the city of Timbuktu these people changed their salt for gold and their gold for salt. Salt was very expensive then! Salt comes through Timbuktu today, but nobody brings any gold.

With all their money, the rich people of Timbuktu made wonderful buildings. You can see a lot of these today, but they are not like other old buildings. People took a lot of soil and then put some water in it. They used this to make beautiful places like the famous

University of Sankore. The people of Timbuktu first made this in the thirteenth century, and the building there now is from 1581.

Students came to the University of Sankore from a lot of different countries. Here they learned about Islam. They also learned to write beautifully. Now there are about 700,000 old papers and books in and near the city of Timbuktu, and some of them come from the twelfth century. You can see a lot of these papers at the famous Ahmed Baba Institute in the city.

In the eighteenth and nineteenth centuries people began to tell stories of Timbuktu in many countries. People from all over Europe wanted to go there, but the roads were long and difficult. Only a small number of visitors arrived at Timbuktu.

Very old books in Timbuktu

The Festival in the Desert

You can go to Timbuktu today by plane or by camel, or you can go along the river Niger and then go a few more kilometres to Timbuktu. When there is a lot of wind, sand from the Sahara Desert blows into the city. But thousands of visitors every year come to see this interesting place in the desert. The famous name of Timbuktu, the beautiful old books, and the wonderful buildings bring them here. And in January each year there is also the *Festival au Désert* – the Festival in the Desert – three days of music in the little village of Essakane, two hours from Timbuktu. You can sit on the sand and hear singers and musicians from Mali and other African countries late into the night. The music of the desert is a new treasure of Timbuktu.

9   Four deserts

Take four deserts: the Sahara in Africa, the Gobi in Asia, the Mojave in North America, and the Atacama in South America. You can find many of the same things in all of these deserts, for example, sand, salt, and rocks. But every desert also has something different – for example, you can only find the famous Bactrian camels in the Gobi.

Let's begin with the world's biggest desert – the Sahara. It is huge at 9,000,000 square kilometres, and it goes across parts of ten different countries in the north of Africa. About 2 million people live here. Some of these are Tuareg and Bedouin people.

The Sahara

The Sahara is a hot desert and the temperatures can be *very* warm in the day. On 13 September 1922 the temperature went up to 57.8 °C in El Azizia in Libya – that's the world's hottest temperature!

The name Sahara comes from the Arabic word for 'desert'. But this part of Africa was not always a desert. There was once a huge sea across the north of Africa – but that was 65 million years ago. Of course, there is not a lot of water there now – half of the Sahara only gets 2 centimetres of rain every year!

Much of the Sahara has small rocks over it and only 15 per cent of the desert is sand. But that sand does not always stay in the Sahara. In 2008, the wind blew a lot of white sand from the Sahara to South Wales in the UK. That's over 1,700 kilometres away!

The huge Gobi Desert in China and Mongolia is over 1,300,000 square kilometres. It is very different from the Sahara because it is a cold desert. In the summer, temperatures can go up to 40 °C but in winter they can go down to -30 °C. It is the best place in the world to see snow in the desert – you can sometimes find up to 15 centimetres of it there.

Mongolian nomads live in this desert and the name Gobi means 'place without water' in their language. Like many traditional desert people, the Mongolian nomads now live an old and a new life. They live in *gers* – big warm tents with beautiful doors. They can easily move these when they need to, usually in spring and autumn. Gers are very traditional, but you can sometimes find new things in them like televisions or computers!

A Mongolian ger

At 57,000 square kilometres, the hot Mojave Desert in California is much smaller than the Sahara and the Gobi. It mostly has dry sand, deep ravines, and big rocks. Death Valley in the Mojave is one of the hottest and driest places in the world. There was the second hottest temperature of all time there on 10 July 1913 at 56.7 °C.

The desert gets its name from the Mojave tribe – these people began to live there hundreds of years ago. Not many people live in the open desert these days, but there are some very big cities here. Las Vegas, with its hotels, big shops, and cinemas, has over 1.9 million people.

Visitors from these cities often go into the Mojave and see the interesting animals and plants there. This desert is famous for its beautiful Joshua trees – you cannot find them in any other place in the world. When people see one, they know they are in the Mojave! In the past, the people of the desert ate the seeds and flowers of the Joshua tree and made shoes from its leaves.

Joshua trees in the Mojave Desert

In most parts of the cool Atacama Desert in Chile you cannot see any trees, because it is one of the driest places in the world. In some parts of the desert there is only rain every 100 years and most places get under 2.5 centimetres every year.

The Atacama is a long desert of 181,300 square kilometres and it is between the Andes mountains and the sea. Much of the desert is up in the tall Andes, so it has cool temperatures from 0 to 25 °C.

Thousands of years ago the Atacama tribe began to live in this desert, and some of them still live there today. In the town of San Miguel de Azapa, you can also see mummies – the dead bodies of people from thousands of years ago. Because of the dry climate, these bodies do not change very much. Some of the Atacama mummies are 9,000 years old.

10   Changes in the desert

Deserts are always changing. After big winds or sudden rain deserts can look very different. They can also get bigger – some deserts like the Sahara and the Thar are growing fast. Places next to these deserts are losing their plants, trees, and water. The wind then blows away the soil and leaves rocks or sand. When the desert grows like this, it is called desertification.

Why does desertification happen? Sometimes it is because of climate change. The world is getting warmer every year and the weather in some places is now different. Changes in the climate can be worse in places next to deserts. With very hot weather and warm winds, these places get very dry. And when there is no water, desertification begins. Because of desertification there is now a new desert in Europe in the part of Romania called Oltenia.

Desertification can happen because of people too. When people take a lot of water from under the desert, the plants begin to die, and the wind blows away the soil. Also, some nomads move about with their goats and camels. The hungry animals eat everything – grass, plants, and trees! Sometimes they leave nothing behind – only the dry desert.

In some places, desertification is very bad. The Gobi Desert is growing fast every year and life is getting difficult for many people. The wind blows sand from the Gobi across China and sometimes into Korea and over the sea to Japan. The desert is now only 160 kilometres from Beijing. Every spring, when the wind blows, all the people in Beijing quickly close their windows and doors!

But people can help to stop desertification. In China, they are beginning to grow a lot of trees next to the Gobi Desert – 2,800 kilometres of them! But this takes a long time – trees do not grow quickly. One day there are going to be big, tall trees there, but not before 2074.

Deserts are also interesting places for visitors. More people are going into the desert because they want to do exciting things, take photos, and look at the animals.

Desertification

In Dubai, you can go in a 4x4 car into the Arabian Desert. First, the driver takes you up and down some big dunes very quickly – this is called dune bashing. After that, you go on a camel for two or three hours. Then you learn about sandboarding. When you go sandboarding, you move very fast down and across the dunes – perhaps at 50 or 60 kilometres an hour. The desert can be an exciting place!

Every year in the Sahara, 700 people run across the desert in the famous *Marathon des Sables* – the Marathon of the Sands. The runners go 240 kilometres in six days. On day four they run about 80 kilometres. The runners also need to carry their things on their backs. It is not easy! But some people want more. For them there is the 4 Deserts Race. There are four races each of 250 kilometres in seven days – in the Atacama, Gobi, and Sahara Deserts, and in Antarctica. Some of the best runners are over 60 years old.

Sandboarding in the Namib

The World Solar Challenge

People also go across the desert in Australia, but there they go in cars. In the World Solar Challenge people from across the world drive 3000 kilometres from the north of Australia to the south. The cars are solar – they work with the help of the sun. The hot desert is a good place for this, and the cars can go fast – up to 130 kilometres an hour.

But what about deserts in the years to come? Some people are beginning to grow plants for food in the desert. These plants bring the desert to life, because you can see huge numbers of green plants next to the dry yellow sand and rocks.

Then there is solar energy. Oil is getting more and more expensive and we need to find energy from other things. In hot deserts people can make lots of energy from the sun. In the Mojave Desert, they make solar energy for houses in different parts of California, and they are also working with solar energy in the Tabernas Desert in Spain.

In the twenty-first century we may need to think again about the huge deserts of the world. Every year there are more and more people on our planet and they all need food and homes. In deserts people can live, play, make energy, and grow food. And in the years to come perhaps deserts are going to be more and more important for the people of the world.

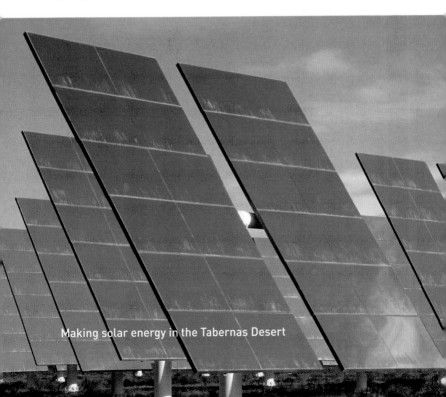

Making solar energy in the Tabernas Desert

GLOSSARY

adapted   changed to work well in a new situation

also   too; as well

blow   to move, or make something move, through the air

century   a time of 100 years

city   a big and important town

climate   the weather you usually get in a certain place

cool   a little cold; between warm and cold

copper   a common metal (Cu) that is red-brown in colour

deep   something that is deep goes down a long way

difficult   not easy to do

dry   with no water in it, or with no rain

energy   power that is used to make electricity, or to make machines work

evaporate   when water evaporates, it changes into a gas and goes into the air

food   what you eat

goat   an animal with horns that gives milk

gold   a yellow metal that is worth a lot of money

grass   a plant with thin green leaves that grows on the ground

grow   to get bigger; to put a plant in the ground and look after it

hole   an empty space or opening in something

huge   very big

Islam   the religion of Muslim people

jump   to move quickly off the ground, using your legs to push you up

leaf (*pl* **leaves**)   one of the flat green parts that grow on a plant or tree

life   the time that you are alive

mountain   a very high hill

music   when you sing or play an instrument, you make music; **musician**   a person who makes music

nose   the part of your face between your mouth and your eyes

oil a thick liquid that comes from under the ground, used for energy

other different

part one of the pieces of something

place where something or somebody is

plant something that grows in the ground

rock something very hard that is found in the ground

root the part of a plant that is under the ground

salt something white that you get from the ground and put on food

sand very small pieces of rock that you find on beaches and in the desert

shopping centre a number of shops built together

snow soft white pieces of frozen water that fall from the sky

soil what plants grow in

story words that tell you about what happened in a certain place or time

temperature how hot or cold something is

traditional when something is traditional, people have done it in the same way for a long time

treasure something that is worth a lot of money

tribe a group of people with the same language who live in a certain place

university a place where people go to study after they leave school

wild wild animals live in nature, not with people

wind air that moves

world the earth with all its countries and people

Deserts

ACTIVITIES

ACTIVITIES

Before Reading

1 **Match the words to the pictures. You can use a dictionary.**

1 ☐ cactus   2 ☐ camel   3 ☐ date palm
4 ☐ dune   5 ☐ lizard   6 ☐ oil

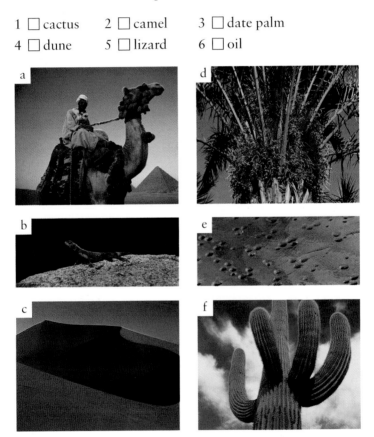

2 **Look back at the words in exercise 1. Answer the questions.**

1 Which of these things have you got in your country?
2 What do you know about these things?

ACTIVITIES

While Reading

Read Chapter 1. Are these sentences true (T) or false (F)? Rewrite the false ones with the correct information.

1 A desert has more than 25 centimetres of rain every year.
2 In 1971, there was some snow in the Atacama Desert.
3 You can sometimes see snow in the Gobi Desert in winter.
4 In the Sahara, the temperatures can go down to -30 °C.
5 The Simpson Desert in Australia is far from the sea.
6 A lot of the desert in the world has small rocks on it.
7 More than one third of the world is desert.

Read Chapter 2, then circle *a*, *b* or *c*.

1 A quarter of the Sahara has got _____ on it.
   a) ravines   b) mountains   c) sand
2 Rivers in the Mojave Desert make the _____ there.
   a) orange sand   b) small hills   c) deep ravines
3 The Gobi Desert in China has a lot of _____.
   a) trees   b) plants   c) rocks
4 The Namib Desert in Africa is famous for its _____.
   a) tall dunes   b) high mountains   c) cold wind
5 The _____ can move sand dunes across the desert.
   a) rain   b) wind   c) desert people
6 Sometimes you can hear a _____ noise from a sand dune.
   a) laughing   b) crying   c) singing
7 The water in an oasis comes from deep _____.
   a) rivers   b) ravines   c) dunes

Read Chapter 3, then match these halves of sentences.

1 Thousands of years ago, the Aborigines began to live . . .
2 Traditional Tuareg families live . . .
3 At night, the San people sleep . . .
4 Families in the Thar Desert in India live . . .
5 The people in Coober Pedy in Australia have got homes . . .
6 Tuareg people wear blue scarves . . .
7 The women of the Thar Desert carry water . . .

a) over their heads and faces.
b) in small homes of trees and plants.
c) under the desert.
d) in bottles on their heads.
e) in the big, dry deserts of Australia.
f) in houses of sand and grass.
g) in huge tents in the desert.

Read Chapter 4, then fill in the gaps with these words.

adapted, eat, goats, oasis, palms, paper daisy, rains, rocks, roots, saguaro cactus, seeds, water

All desert plants are _____ to dry weather and they can live without much _____. Many desert plants have huge _____ – these sometimes go down deep into the _____.

Desert plants like the famous _____ live for a very long time – sometimes 200 years! But others like the _____ only live for a short time. They leave their _____ in the sand and only come to life when it _____.

Date _____ are important for desert people and you can find them near an _____. People _____ the dates or give them to their _____ and other animals.

Read Chapter 5 then complete the sentences with words from the list below.

Bactrian, Dromedary, Fennec foxes, Jerboas, Scorpions

1 _____ can jump up to three metres.
2 _____ camels have two humps and live wild in the Gobi.
3 _____ can live for one year without food.
4 _____ have very big ears and white coats.
5 _____ camels have one hump and do not live wild in deserts.

Read Chapter 6. Choose the best question-word for these questions, and then answer them.

How many / What / Where / Who / Why

1 . . . do most Bedouins live now?
2 . . . is the most important person in a Bedouin tribe?
3 . . . do visitors drink when they are with the Bedouins?
4 . . . nights can a visitor stay with the Bedouins?
5 . . . do the Bedouins drink when they are ill?
6 . . . is the twenty-first century difficult for the Bedouins?

Read Chapter 7, then rewrite these untrue sentences with the correct information.

1 Thousands of years ago, nomads looked for rivers in the Sahara.
2 In Mali, people put eight big pieces of salt onto every camel.
3 People found oil under the Arabian Desert in the 1950s.
4 A lot of the world's oil is in the Atacama Desert in Chile.
5 The huge mine in Chile is 4.5 kilometres wide.
6 People need salt to make bottles and windows.

Read Chapter 8, then circle the correct words.

1 Riyadh is much *smaller* / *bigger* than Alice Springs.

2 Long ago, Timbuktu was a very *rich* / *poor* town.

3 In Timbuktu people changed salt for *camels* / *gold*.

4 People used *sand* / *soil* to make the buildings in Timbuktu.

5 A lot of people came to *study* / *eat* in the city.

6 The Festival in the Desert is a *music* / *book* festival.

Read Chapter 9. Complete these sentences with the name of one of these deserts: *Atacama*, *Gobi*, *Mojave* or *Sahara*.

1 The _____ Desert is one of the driest places in the world.

2 You can only find Joshua trees in the _____ Desert.

3 The _____ Desert is the world's biggest desert.

4 Nomads in the _____ Desert live in *gers*.

5 You can find very old mummies in the _____ Desert.

6 The very hot, dry Death Valley is in the _____ Desert.

7 You can sometimes find snow in the _____ Desert.

8 The world's hottest temperature was in the _____ Desert.

Read Chapter 10, then answer these questions.

1 What is the word for when deserts grow bigger?

2 Where is the new desert in Europe?

3 Where does the wind blow the sand from the Gobi Desert?

4 What are people doing to stop desertification in China?

5 What is dune bashing?

6 Where do people run in the 4 Deserts Race?

7 What are people beginning to grow in some deserts?

ACTIVITIES

After Reading

1 **Complete the crossword.**

ACROSS:

1 A very big bird – it eats dead animals.

4 People keep this animal for its milk and its hair.

5 Very small pieces of rock.

6 A very dangerous insect that lives in hot countries.

10 A long deep hole that goes across the desert.

11 A big hole in the ground where people get gold or salt.

12 The part of a plant that goes down into the soil.

DOWN:

2 People sleep in this cloth house when they go camping.

3 A place in the desert where you can find water.

5 You wear this over your head or round your neck.

7 A metal that is a red-brown colour.

8 Something white that comes from the ground; you put it on your food.

9 In cold weather, these soft white things fall from the sky.

2 Complete these two postcards using the words below.

backs, camels, city, colours, homes, mine, rich, rock, salt, sand, soil, temperature, under, University, unusual, wind

---

Dear Lily

I'm in Timbuktu – the most famous desert _____ in the world!

Long ago, it was a very _____ town and people made beautiful buildings from _____ and water – isn't that wonderful? The _____ of Sankore from 1581 is the most important one, I think.

This morning, we saw some huge _____ with _____ from the Sahara on their _____. But later, the _____ suddenly began to blow _____ into the streets from the Sahara and we all ran back to our hotel!

love

Amy

Dear Dominic

We're in Coober Pedy in South Australia. It's a really _____ town – a lot of the _____ are built down in the _____. We're staying in the Desert Cave hotel and our rooms are right _____ the desert. It's nice and cool there and the _____ is about 24 °C. Outside it's sometimes 40 °C!

Coober Pedy is famous for its opals – beautiful stones of many _____ from under the ground. Tomorrow we're going to visit an opal _____.

See you soon

Simon

3 You are going on a visit to a desert. Answer these questions, and then discuss your answers with a partner.

1 Which desert in the world are you going to visit? Why?

2 What things are you going to take with you?

3 How are you going to travel?

4 Where are you going to sleep at night?

5 What are you going to see and do?

4 Read Chapter 9 again. Copy the table and make notes about the different deserts.

	Sahara	Gobi	Mojave	Atacama
Size	9,000,000 square km.			
Location	North Africa.			
Name	Comes from the Arabic word for 'desert'.			
People	Tuaregs and Bedouins.			
Desert type	Hot desert.			
Landscape	Rocks and sand.			
Interesting fact	It had the world's hottest temperature.			

Find out about another desert. Give a talk to your class about it. You can get more information from websites like www.wikipedia.org and www.livingdesert.org.

ABOUT THE AUTHOR

Janet Hardy-Gould is an experienced teacher, writer, and teacher trainer. She is married with two children and lives in the ancient town of Lewes in the south of England. She has worked extensively on activities and support materials for OUP readers, notably for the Dominoes series and the Oxford Bookworms Library, and has published titles in both series. Her other Bookworms titles are *King Arthur* (Human Interest) and *Henry VIII and his Six Wives* (True Stories). In her free time, she likes walking across the beautiful hills near her town and meeting friends in cafés for tea and cakes.

Janet has lived and taught in both France and Spain and loves travelling. Since crossing the vast deserts of the United States some years ago, she has remained fascinated with desert life – the people, the plants and particularly the animals. One of her favourite places is the reptile house at the world-famous London Zoo, where there are many wonderful examples of desert animals.

OXFORD BOOKWORMS LIBRARY

Classics • Crime & Mystery • Factfiles • Fantasy & Horror
Human Interest • Playscripts • Thriller & Adventure
True Stories • World Stories

The OXFORD BOOKWORMS LIBRARY provides enjoyable reading in English, with a wide range of classic and modern fiction, non-fiction, and plays. It includes original and adapted texts in seven carefully graded language stages, which take learners from beginner to advanced level. An overview is given on the next pages.

All Stage 1 titles are available as audio recordings, as well as over eighty other titles from Starter to Stage 6. All Starters and many titles at Stages 1 to 4 are specially recommended for younger learners. Every Bookworm is illustrated, and Starters and Factfiles have full-colour illustrations.

The OXFORD BOOKWORMS LIBRARY also offers extensive support. Each book contains an introduction to the story, notes about the author, a glossary, and activities. Additional resources include tests and worksheets, and answers for these and for the activities in the books. There is advice on running a class library, using audio recordings, and the many ways of using Oxford Bookworms in reading programmes. Resource materials are available on the website <www.oup.com/bookworms>.

The *Oxford Bookworms Collection* is a series for advanced learners. It consists of volumes of short stories by well-known authors, both classic and modern. Texts are not abridged or adapted in any way, but carefully selected to be accessible to the advanced student.

You can find details and a full list of titles in the *Oxford Bookworms Library Catalogue* and *Oxford English Language Teaching Catalogues*, and on the website <www.oup.com/bookworms>.

THE OXFORD BOOKWORMS LIBRARY
GRADING AND SAMPLE EXTRACTS

STARTER • 250 HEADWORDS

present simple – present continuous – imperative –
can/cannot, must – *going to* (future) – simple gerunds ...

Her phone is ringing – but where is it?

Sally gets out of bed and looks in her bag. No phone. She looks under the bed. No phone. Then she looks behind the door. There is her phone. Sally picks up her phone and answers it. *Sally's Phone*

STAGE 1 • 400 HEADWORDS

... past simple – coordination with *and, but, or* –
subordination with *before, after, when, because, so* ...

I knew him in Persia. He was a famous builder and I worked with him there. For a time I was his friend, but not for long. When he came to Paris, I came after him – I wanted to watch him. He was a very clever, very dangerous man. *The Phantom of the Opera*

STAGE 2 • 700 HEADWORDS

... present perfect – *will* (future) – *(don't) have to, must not, could* –
comparison of adjectives – simple *if* clauses – past continuous –
tag questions – *ask/tell* + infinitive ...

While I was writing these words in my diary, I decided what to do. I must try to escape. I shall try to get down the wall outside. The window is high above the ground, but I have to try. I shall take some of the gold with me – if I escape, perhaps it will be helpful later. *Dracula*

STAGE 3 • 1000 HEADWORDS

… should, may – present perfect continuous – *used to* – past perfect
– causative – relative clauses – indirect statements …

Of course, it was most important that no one should see Colin, Mary, or Dickon entering the secret garden. So Colin gave orders to the gardeners that they must all keep away from that part of the garden in future. *The Secret Garden*

STAGE 4 • 1400 HEADWORDS

… past perfect continuous – passive (simple forms) –
would conditional clauses – indirect questions –
relatives with *where/when* – gerunds after prepositions/phrases …

I was glad. Now Hyde could not show his face to the world again. If he did, every honest man in London would be proud to report him to the police. *Dr Jekyll and Mr Hyde*

STAGE 5 • 1800 HEADWORDS

… future continuous – future perfect –
passive (modals, continuous forms) –
would have conditional clauses – modals + perfect infinitive …

If he had spoken Estella's name, I would have hit him. I was so angry with him, and so depressed about my future, that I could not eat the breakfast. Instead I went straight to the old house. *Great Expectations*

STAGE 6 • 2500 HEADWORDS

… passive (infinitives, gerunds) – advanced modal meanings –
clauses of concession, condition

When I stepped up to the piano, I was confident. It was as if I knew that the prodigy side of me really did exist. And when I started to play, I was so caught up in how lovely I looked that I didn't worry how I would sound. *The Joy Luck Club*

BOOKWORMS · FACTFILES · STAGE 1

Animals in Danger

ANDY HOPKINS AND JOC POTTER

People love and need animals. They keep them in their homes and on their farms. They enjoy going to zoos, and watching animals on films and on TV. Little children love to play with toy animals.

But people are a great danger to animals too. They take their land, and cut down the trees where animals have their homes. They pollute the rivers and seas, and kill big animals for their skins or for medicine. Now there are about 7,000 species of animals in danger. What can we do to protect the animals of the world – from us?

BOOKWORMS · FACTFILES · STAGE 2

Climate Change

BARNABY NEWBOLT

It's a terrible problem – or it's really not as bad as people say. There will be sudden big changes – or slower changes that we can learn to live with. It means the end for many animals, people, even whole islands – but will this happen soon, or hundreds of years from now?

What is the true story about climate change? Why is it happening, and what can we do about it? If we learn about the past, then perhaps there will be time to make changes for the future . . .